Original title:
Quiet Liberation

Copyright © 2024 Swan Charm
All rights reserved.

Author: Olivia Oja
ISBN HARDBACK: 978-9908-1-2488-9
ISBN PAPERBACK: 978-9908-1-2489-6
ISBN EBOOK: 978-9908-1-2490-2

Tranquil Resurgence

In the heart of the night, stars softly gleam,
Laughter spills over like a warm, flowing stream.
Colors dance brightly, a vivid array,
Joy fills the air, as we welcome the day.

Candles are flickering, shadows at play,
Hand in hand, we chase worries away.
Songs echo sweetly, a melodious tide,
Together we stand, with hearts open wide.

Tables adorned with delights, oh so bright,
Gathered in friendship, embraced by the light.
Smiles and warm hugs, a festival's grace,
In this tranquil moment, we find our place.

As the moon takes its throne, we savor the cheer,
Every wish whispered, brings loved ones near.
With each gentle toast, our spirits arise,
In this tranquil resurgence, our hearts touch the skies.

Eclipsed Chains

Bright lights dance in the night,
    Joy echoes in every heart,
    Colors swirl, a vivid sight,
    Together, we will not part.

Chains of doubt now fade away,
    Laughter fills the open air,
In this moment, come what may,
Together, we're beyond compare.

Whispered Awakening

Soft whispers beckon us near,
In the glow of dawn's embrace,
Hearts alight, we cast out fear,
Hope and joy, a shared space.

With each note, the world is bright,
Laughter spills like morning dew,
In this dance, the spirit's flight,
Every moment feels anew.

Lush Solitude

In the garden where colors blaze,
Petals dance in the sun's warm rays.
Breezes whisper soft and sweet,
Life's simple joys, a rhythmic beat.

Friends gather round with laughter bright,
Under the stars' enchanting light.
Joyful moments, shared with grace,
Time stands still in this magic place.

The Sound of Release

Drums echo through the vibrant night,
In every heartbeat, pure delight.
Voices soar like birds in flight,
Freedom found in the soft moonlight.

Fingers snap with rhythmic cheer,
Melodies that draw us near.
Feet on fire, we move as one,
Underneath the laughing sun.

The Ties that Unravel

Kites in the sky, dancing on air,
Strings released, without a care.
Every thread tells a story bold,
Of dreams and wishes yet untold.

Hands reach out in a playful game,
Celebrating life, never the same.
Laughter weaves through the fragrant field,
In this moment, our hearts revealed.

Harmony in Hush

Under the twilight's gentle embrace,
Whispers of joy weave through space.
Candles flicker, casting soft glow,
A serene path where spirits flow.

The hush of night invites us in,
Where laughter echoes, and dreams begin.
Each moment savored, a treasure deep,
In this festive calm, our hearts leap.

The Calm of Release

Under the stars, laughter flows,
Balloons drift high, as joy grows.
Warm embraces, friends unite,
In this moment, hearts take flight.

Candles flicker, sweet scents rise,
Gifts of love wrapped in surprise.
Soft music plays, a gentle hum,
In the calm, our souls succumb.

Embrace of the Unseen

Colors spark in twilight air,
Lively smiles everywhere.
Whispers of joy dance around,
In the unseen, love is found.

Shadowed corners hold delight,
Mysterious twinkles glow bright.
Together we share this night,
In warm embrace, hearts feel light.

The Subtle Euphony

Chimes of laughter, soft and clear,
Melodies of joy draw near.
Each note a thread, weaving tight,
In harmony, we find our light.

Footsteps mingle, a rhythmic beat,
Dancing spirits, feel the heat.
In this symphony of cheer,
Every heartbeat sings, sincere.

Quiet Crescendos

In the hush, excitement brews,
Gentle whispers, evening hues.
As shadows stretch, the night awakes,
With each turn, the laughter shakes.

Stars align in playful jest,
In this calm, we find our best.
Quiet crescendos rise and swell,
In joyous hearts, our stories tell.

Emancipation Through Quietude

In the hush of twilight glow,
Joy dances in the shadows low.
Laughter echoes, sweet and clear,
Freedom whispers, drawing near.

Beneath the stars, we spin and sway,
In the soft embrace of end of day.
Hearts united, light ablaze,
In quietude, our spirits raise.

Solace in Shadows

Beneath the trees where soft winds sigh,
We gather 'neath the painted sky.
The world outside may seem so bright,
Yet here we find our pure delight.

In whispers soft and laughter shared,
A tapestry of love declared.
Within the shadows, joy does bloom,
Creating light within the gloom.

The Unheard Symphony

In the silence, melodies rise,
A symphony beneath the skies.
Each note a story, softly spun,
In every heartbeat, life has won.

Amidst the chaos, joy does play,
With every breath, we find our way.
An unheard symphony we create,
In unity, we celebrate.

Embracing the Empty Spaces

In the silence, there's a song,
In the stillness, we belong.
Empty spaces hold their grace,
Festive cheer in every place.

With open hearts, we dare to dream,
Finding joy in every gleam.
In the pauses, magic gleans,
Embracing all the in-betweens.

Unseen Wings

In gardens bright, laughter sways,
Balloons drift high on sunny days.
Whispers of joy fill the air,
As love and friendship find their share.

Dancing shadows, gleeful fleet,
A symphony of heartbeats sweet.
Unseen wings lift spirits high,
With dreams that flutter, dance, and fly.

Gentle Release

With stars that twinkle, spirits rise,
The moonlight casts its silver ties.
Laughter lingers, soft and clear,
As waves of joy draw everyone near.

Colors burst like fireworks bright,
Filling the dark with pure delight.
A gentle release, hearts unite,
In the embrace of the magical night.

Unburdened Dawn

A new day breaks, the world awakes,
With golden hues that warmth creates.
Birds in chorus sing their cheer,
In this moment, all is clear.

Tangled thoughts now drift away,
Replaced by hope, the sun's soft ray.
Unburdened dawn, fresh and bold,
Unfolding stories yet untold.

The Hush of Awakening

In soft stillness, the world begins,
With gentle breezes, nature spins.
The hush of awakening calls us near,
As dreams and hopes now reappear.

Flowers bloom, a fragrant sigh,
Underneath the vast blue sky.
In every heartbeat, joy takes flight,
As we embrace this pure delight.

Unseen Wings

In the air, laughter soars,
Colors dance, a sweet embrace.
Balloons rise, hearts ignite,
Joyful whispers fill the space.

Candles flicker, wishes bloom,
Friends and family gather near.
Mirthful songs chase away gloom,
Infinite love, we hold dear.

Glistening lights twinkle bright,
Harmony in every cheer.
Moments shared, our spirits light,
Together, we find our cheer.

Unseen wings lift our souls,
Celebration in full swing.
Hope and laughter make us whole,
In this dance, we take flight.

Tranquil Resurgence

Softly falls the autumn rain,
Whispers of the past emerge.
Nature sings in gentle strains,
Renewed spirit starts to surge.

Golden leaves in breezy sway,
Echoes of a joyful time.
As we breathe the day away,
Peaceful rhythms, gentle rhyme.

Chairs around the fire glow,
Faces warm with love and light.
Voices share what we both know,
In this harmony, we unite.

Rivers flow with soothing grace,
Moments linger, softly glide.
Together, we find our place,
In the calm where dreams reside.

The Art of Letting Go

In the stillness of the night,
Stars fall gently from the sky.
Embracing all that feels so right,
In this freedom, we can fly.

Old regrets like autumn leaves,
Drift away on whispered breeze.
With each breath, our spirit frees,
Letting go, we find our ease.

Laughter rings like silver chimes,
Hands released, we twirl around.
Every moment softly climbs,
In this joy, we are unbound.

From the past, we take a bow,
Opening our hearts anew.
Grateful for each precious now,
In the light, we start to view.

Shadows of Peace

Beneath the moon's serene glow,
Silhouettes of dreams take flight.
In the stillness, moments flow,
Whispers cradled by the night.

Candles flicker, secrets shared,
In the shadows, we reflect.
Hearts laid bare, no fear, no cared,
Finding love in every aspect.

Hope cascades like a gentle stream,
Filling spaces once felt cold.
Together weaving every dream,
In this tapestry, we're bold.

From quiet minds, new joys arise,
While the world hums soft and deep.
In these moments, hear the sighs,
Shadows hold the peace we keep.

Whispers of Freedom

The sun spills gold on fields of cheer,
Where laughter dances, bright and clear.
Joyful hearts rise, a vibrant song,
In every moment, we all belong.

Colorful banners flutter in the breeze,
Sharing secrets with rustling leaves.
Together we twirl, hand in hand,
Under the sky, a joyous land.

The air is sweet with a fragrant bloom,
Echoes of hope fill every room.
Chasing shadows of sorrow away,
In this festive light, we choose to stay.

Freedom rings in the vibrant night,
Stars above, our guiding light.
Together we'll dream, together we'll sing,
In the whispers of freedom, our spirits take wing.

Stillness Unbound

In twilight's embrace, we find our peace,
Where moments linger, time may cease.
A gentle hush wraps around the night,
In the stillness, everything feels right.

Candles flicker with a warm, soft glow,
Reflecting on faces, love's overflow.
Each heartbeat echoes in rhythmic rhyme,
In this sacred space, we stall time.

The world stands still, drifting in dreams,
Wrapped in whispers, and soft moonbeams.
Laughter reverberates, a sweet refrain,
In the stillness, joy breaks every chain.

Together we bask in this calming sight,
Hearts intertwined, spirits alight.
In the stillness unbound, our souls unite,
Creating memories that feel just right.

The Beauty of Dusk

As the day begins to wane,
Stars emerge with gentle grace,
Moments cherished, free from pain,
In this twilight, find your place.

Candles flicker, warmth remains,
Songs of joy, we sing aloud,
In each laugh, a sweet refrain,
Together, we are so proud.

Surrendered Stillness

In the quiet, magic stirs,
Silence wraps the world in peace,
The heart's rhythm softly purrs,
In this calm, we find release.

Gentle moments, sweetly shared,
Every breath a cherished gift,
In this space, our souls have bared,
Together, let our spirits lift.

The Sound of Solitude

Silent moments breathe with grace,
Each thought unfurls, a gentle embrace.
In the quiet, whispers softly play,
Creating beauty in their own way.

Alone but not lonely, we happily roam,
Finding treasures in the spaces we comb.
A symphony of echoes fills the air,
In solitude's heart, we discover care.

The rustle of leaves, a soothing sound,
Nature speaks softly, our spirits unbound.
With each quiet pause, we learn to see,
The harmony within, what it means to be.

In the sound of solitude, we find our way,
Embracing the stillness of night and day.
With joy in our hearts, we're never alone,
In the depths of silence, our souls are shown.

Echoes of Serenity

Underneath a sky of twilight blue,
The world transforms, each moment anew.
Serenity flows like a calm, soft stream,
Carrying wishes, wrapped in a dream.

A tapestry woven with threads of light,
Colors bloom in the fading night.
In tranquil whispers, we find our way,
Guided by starlight's gentle sway.

The laughter of friends lifts spirits high,
Echoes of joy dancing in the sky.
Together we share in this wondrous peace,
In the sanctuary of moments, we find release.

As the moon cradles the day in goodbye,
We gather our dreams, letting worries fly.
In the echoes of serenity, our hearts align,
In this perfect stillness, we truly shine.

Transcendence in Solitude

In quiet realms where spirits soar,
The stars above ignite and roar.
A gentle breeze whispers delight,
In solitude, we find our light.

Moments pause, a world anew,
Where dreams take flight, and shadows strew.
Each heartbeat echoes through the night,
Embracing peace, our hearts ignite.

Soft Shadows Dance

Beneath the moon, soft shadows sway,
In rhythms bright, they twirl and play.
A shimmering glow, a curtain drawn,
As twilight sings the hush of dawn.

The laughter echoes, warm and clear,
With every step, our joys draw near.
Embracing warmth, we weave our glee,
In soft shadows, wild and free.

Voices of the Unheard

In the silence, voices rise,
Painting visions in the skies.
With courage born from hidden strife,
They sing the tales of vibrant life.

The melodies break through the night,
A chorus born of pure delight.
Each whisper carried on the breeze,
Uplifting spirits, hearts at ease.

Unraveled Threads

In tapestries of joy and cheer,
Unraveled threads begin to clear.
Colors blend in a festive hue,
In every knot, a tale rings true.

As laughter weaves through every seam,
Together we create a dream.
With every stitch, our stories blend,
A vibrant patchwork that won't end.

Silent Vows

Underneath the twinkling lights,
Whispers float like gentle sighs.
Hearts entwined in soft delight,
Promises made beneath the skies.

Laughter dances on the breeze,
Joyful love in every glance.
Together we will seize,
This moment—a sweet romance.

Candles glow with warmth and cheer,
As friendships gather all around.
In this space, we hold dear,
Silent vows in joy abound.

The night unfolds, a vibrant dream,
With every voice, a song to share.
Side by side, we form a team,
Together, we dissolve despair.

Embracing the Void

In shadows deep, a spark ignites,
Colors bloom in radiant waves.
Dancing dreams through starry nights,
In darkness, a light that saves.

Echoes of laughter fill the air,
Filling hearts with hope and grace.
Together, we embrace despair,
Creating joy within this space.

We twirl like leaves, alight and free,
Each moment cherished, not lost.
In every heart, a jubilee,
A festive joy that pays the cost.

As we step boldly into night,
Hand in hand, we face the void.
With every heartbeat, pure delight,
In unity, our fears destroyed.

Freedom's Gentle Touch

Whispers soft on summer's breath,
The sun ignites the skies so bright.
In every heartbeat, life and death,
We celebrate the day and night.

Fields of gold, the flowers sway,
Laughter spills from young and old.
In every dance, a wild play,
A tapestry of stories told.

With open arms, we greet the dawn,
A canvas fresh for dreams to paint.
With every note, our worries gone,
In freedom's touch, we feel no restraint.

So let us dance beneath the stars,
With spirits high, we rise and sing.
Embracing life, from near to far,
In unity, the joy we bring.

The Calm Before the Storm

The air is still, a hush profound,
As twilight whispers through the trees.
In quiet moments, peace is found,
A soothing calm, a gentle breeze.

But sparkles dance upon the tide,
With clouds that hint at coming thrill.
In every heart, the wild resides,
A spark of joy, unknown until.

Eager eyes glance at the sky,
Awaiting wonders that will burst.
In silence, we breathe a sigh,
And feel the pulse of joy—the first.

For storms bring life, a vibrant thrill,
Through raindrops, laughter weaves its way.
In chaos, hearts begin to fill,
With memories of a bright array.

Muted Resurgence

In twilight's glow, the lanterns sway,
Colors burst, as night turns to day.
Laughter dances on the soft breeze,
Joyful hearts, for now, are at ease.

With each step, rhythms arise,
Dreams ignited, under starry skies.
A chorus of voices fills the air,
Hope rekindled, everywhere.

Festival lights, they twinkle bright,
Breaking shadows, bringing light.
Embracing moments, side by side,
In this warmth, we take pride.

Through muted echoes, spirits soar,
Whispers of love, forever more.
In this night, our spirits blend,
A muted resurgence, without end.

Whispers of the Unbound

In gardens wild, the flowers hum,
Sweet melodies, a joyful drum.
Colors radiate, moments unfold,
Whispers of stories, waiting to be told.

Banners flutter, painted bright,
Under the canopy, pure delight.
Together we gather, hearts afire,
Fueling the spirit, lifting us higher.

Voices merge in a happy song,
Embracing everyone, rich and strong.
In laughter's embrace, we find our place,
The whispers of the unbound, we chase.

With every smile, the world ignites,
Shimmering stars, enchanting nights.
In unity, let our worries fade,
Joy's sweet anthem, serenely played.

Silent Horizons

As sun dips low, the sky ignites,
Painting dreams in vibrant sights.
Gathered hands, a circle round,
In silence shared, our hopes are found.

The gentle breeze, it calls our name,
Carrying whispers, kindling flame.
With every glance, our spirits meet,
In this moment, life feels sweet.

Horizon glows, a canvas bright,
Forging bonds in the fading light.
Together, we bask in twilight's embrace,
Our hearts intertwine in this sacred space.

In silent harmony, we stand tall,
Echoes of laughter, a festival call.
Through shared dreams, our spirits rise,
Silent horizons, endless skies.

Veils of Silence

A hush descends, the night begins,
Softly it lingers, like gentle spins.
Behind the veils, the magic waits,
A tapestry woven, through open gates.

In the shadows, sparks ignite,
A dance of joy beneath the light.
Faces glowing, a painted scene,
Together we weave, a vibrant dream.

The world awakens, with whispers sweet,
In every heartbeat, we feel the beat.
Through the silence, connections bloom,
In the night's embrace, dispelling gloom.

Veils of silence, where dreams reside,
In our laughter, hope will guide.
A festival of souls, we celebrate,
In the stillness, we elevate.

When Stillness Speaks

In the glow of twilight's cheer,
Whispers dance on breezy air,
Laughter floats like fireflies bright,
As hearts are light, devoid of care.

Bells ring out through joyful streets,
Each note a promise, pure and sweet,
Colors burst in vibrant hues,
The world in sync, our souls enthuse.

Festive songs fill open skies,
Children play with gleeful cries,
Moments shared in happy cheer,
When stillness speaks, all draws near.

So let us join this merry throng,
In celebration, we belong,
With every smile, our spirits soar,
When stillness speaks, we seek for more.

Liberation in Lullabies

Under stars, the world unwinds,
Hushed whispers with gentle winds,
Dreams take flight on silken wings,
In lullabies, true freedom sings.

Candles flicker, shadows play,
A vibrant dance, both night and day,
Each note a thread of magic spun,
In harmony, we become as one.

Time stands still, the worries fade,
In this moment, love displayed,
Together wrapped in soft embrace,
Liberation found in this space.

As moonlight drapes in silver gown,
We lose our fears, we wear no crown,
In lullabies, our hearts unite,
And celebrate the joy of night.

Unspoken Promises

In laughter's echo, secrets bloom,
A spark ignites within the room,
Silent vows weave through the air,
Unspoken promises we share.

With every glance, connections grow,
A dance of hearts, a subtle flow,
The night unfolds its tender grace,
In joyful pauses, we find our place.

Around the fire, stories unfold,
Warmth envelops, as dreams unfold,
With every sigh, a cheer takes flight,
In whispered truths, we find our light.

Together under starry skies,
We cherish moments, never disguise,
Unspoken bonds that tie us tight,
In festive hearts, we find our light.

The Freedom Found in Stillness

When bustling days begin to fade,
In gentle quiet, peace is laid,
A moment's pause, a breath bestowed,
The freedom found in silence glowed.

Stars align in perfect grace,
In stillness, we discover space,
To breathe, to dream, to simply be,
A festive spirit, wild and free.

The world resounds with joyful sound,
Yet in stillness, joy is found,
A dance of thoughts, a tranquil song,
In freedom's embrace, we all belong.

So let us cherish this retreat,
In stillness, life feels more complete,
For in that hush, we come alive,
The freedom found, where hearts arrive.

Beneath the Surface

Beneath the waves, joy glimmers bright,
Colors dance in the soft moonlight.
Laughter bubbles up from the deep,
Secrets of the ocean, in silence, we keep.

Shells whisper stories of long ago,
Echoes of parties from the flow.
Fish weave in and out a merry sight,
Under the tide, a world of delight.

Beneath the surface, magic runs wild,
In every corner, a playful child.
Water's embrace, cool and alive,
In this hidden realm, we all thrive.

The Lightness of Being

In the air, laughter swirls and twirls,
Joy igniting a dance of pearls.
Feet lift off the ground with glee,
The weight of the world, we finally flee.

Blissful moments, like feathers in flight,
Carry our spirits into the night.
With every heartbeat, a rhythm pure,
In this lightness, we find our cure.

Joy spills over, refreshing and bright,
Celebrations ring out in warm twilight.
Together we stand, hearts open wide,
In the lightness of being, we take pride.

Cheering the Quiet

In the stillness, cheer begins to bloom,
Soft whispers fill up the room.
Stars above peek shy and bright,
In the calm, we find our light.

Candles flicker with a gentle glow,
As we gather, our hearts shall show.
In the quiet, joy does reign,
Simple moments, profound, not in vain.

Toasting softly under the night,
Celebrating peace, our hearts take flight.
In every silence, a song unfolds,
Cheering the quiet, our love retold.

Embrace the Silence

In the hush of evening, dreams take flight,
Wrapped in stillness, our worries light.
Each heartbeat whispers a soft refrain,
Embracing silence, we break the chain.

Moonbeams dance on the calm lake's edge,
Inviting us close, a gentle pledge.
With every breath, we find our grace,
In tranquil spaces, we find our place.

Together we sit, quiet yet bold,
Treasures of silence, purest gold.
With open hearts, let the stillness sing,
Embrace the silence, let joy take wing.

The Breath of Deep Waters

Beneath the waves, the colors play,
Dancing light in a gentle sway.
Echoes of laughter rise and fall,
Nature's joy, a festive call.

Shells and treasures, secrets to find,
Waves caress with a rhythm kind.
The salty breeze sings a sweet tune,
Under the warm embrace of the moon.

Children giggle, splashing with glee,
As tides bring gifts from the vast sea.
With each wave that kisses the shore,
Memories made, and spirits soar.

A canvas bright, painted with cheer,
In this moment, nothing to fear.
The breath of waters, deep and clear,
Whispers of joy that we hold dear.

Escape through Stillness

In the quiet, a gentle hum,
Nature's heartbeat, a soothing drum.
Leaves flutter softly in vibrant hues,
A festivity wrapped in morning dew.

Sunlight spills like liquid gold,
Stories of warmth in whispers told.
Beneath the boughs, we find our peace,
Time stands still, and worries cease.

Petals dance on the fragrant air,
Breathless beauty everywhere.
We share a smile, a fleeting glance,
In stillness, we find sweet romance.

With every sigh, the spirit lifts,
Nature's embrace, her joyful gifts.
In the stillness, we feel alive,
A festive hush, where dreams can thrive.

Whispers of the Heart

In the twilight glow, sparks ignite,
As laughter dances through the night.
With every heartbeat, joy unfolds,
Whispers of warmth as stories are told.

Beneath the stars, a canvas wide,
Friendship woven, side by side.
The gentle breeze carries our song,
In this embrace, we all belong.

Moments linger like sweet perfume,
In the air, a festive tune.
Each glance an echo, a tender spark,
Binding our souls, lighting the dark.

With hands held tight, we chase the dawn,
In this sweet symphony, we are drawn.
Whispers of joy, with every breath,
Celebrating life, defying death.

The Serene Ascent

Up the hillside, our spirits rise,
With every step, we touch the skies.
The world below, a jubilant place,
As we climb higher, we find our grace.

Colors burst in a lively display,
Nature celebrates in her own way.
With laughter echoing through the trees,
The festive air floats on the breeze.

At the summit, we pause to breathe,
In this stillness, our hearts believe.
The laughter shared, the views we see,
In this moment, we feel so free.

With arms outstretched, we embrace the sun,
In this serene space, we are one.
The ascent a journey, a joyful climb,
With every heartbeat, we feel the rhyme.

Lullaby of the Untethered

Stars twinkle bright in a velvet night,
Whispers of joy take flight,
Colors dance, hearts ignite,
In this space, we find our light.

Laughter spills like wine,
Melodies sweetly entwine,
Freedom sings, oh so divine,
Together we gleam and shine.

Banners wave in the breeze,
Every spirit at ease,
As we sway beneath the trees,
In this moment, life's a tease.

So let the music play,
Chasing our cares away,
In this festive, bright array,
Together we greet the day.

Stillness Unchained

In the glow of lanterns fair,
Dreams unfold, hearts laid bare,
Spirit of joy fills the air,
Unity found everywhere.

Voices hum a gentle tune,
Underneath the silver moon,
In this stillness, we'll commune,
As the night sings our sweet boon.

Hands held tight in warm embrace,
Every smile a cherished trace,
In this magic, time slows its pace,
Every moment's filled with grace.

So let the night be bright,
With laughter shared in pure delight,
Together we own this right,
In stillness, we feel the light.

The Soft Rebellion

A tapestry of colors spun,
Under the glare of the setting sun,
Where hearts beat as one,
And love's bright spark has begun.

With every step, we break the mold,
Stories of joy gently told,
In this warmth, we find the bold,
Unity in dreams of gold.

Beneath the stars, we raise our voice,
In this revelry, we rejoice,
Together here, we make the choice,
To celebrate, to feel, to poise.

So let the music start,
With every note, heal a heart,
In this joyful art,
We rise, we play our part.

Hidden Horizons

The dawn breaks with gentle cheer,
Colors burst, the sky is clear,
Every moment, we draw near,
To dreams hidden yet sincere.

In the market, laughter rings,
Celebrations and offerings,
Joyful hearts as freedom sings,
Together we embrace the flings.

Through the fields, we wander wide,
With smiles shared, hearts open wide,
In this moment, let's confide,
In the laughter, our dreams reside.

So let the day unfold,
With stories shared and joy retold,
In this fest, both brave and bold,
Together, our lives we hold.

Softly Unfurling

Balloons dance in the warm, bright air,
Laughter twirls, we gather everywhere.
Colors burst with joyful delight,
Dreams take flight under the soft moonlight.

Candles flicker, glowing faces shine,
Each moment a treasure, so sweetly divine.
Voices blend in a melodic song,
Together we laugh, where all hearts belong.

Fairy lights twinkle, stars in our eyes,
Time slows down beneath the vast skies.
The night whispers tales of love and cheer,
As friendships flourish, bold and sincere.

Sweets and treats beckon from every stall,
Joy unites us, we embrace it all.
A tapestry woven of hearts entwined,
In this festive realm, true peace we find.

Emancipation in Shadows

Candlelit corners cradle soft sighs,
In whispered dreams, our spirit flies.
Masks are lifted, truth takes its stand,
Together we rise, hand in hand.

The music swirls, shadows begin to sway,
Our souls break free, casting fears away.
Each heartbeat pulses like a radiant drum,
In this dance of joy, our spirits become.

Confetti rains down, a burst of gold,
Stories are shared, both timid and bold.
Laughter rings clear, like bells in the night,
In this sanctuary, everything feels right.

We celebrate life, in all that it brings,
A symphony of hope, as freedom sings.
Under the starlit embrace, we transcend,
In the dance of shadows, there's no end.

Tranquil Escape

Gentle breezes whisper through the trees,
Sunset hues paint the sky with ease.
A peaceful retreat where worries fade,
In nature's arms, we find our aid.

Footsteps soft on the mossy ground,
In stillness profound, solace is found.
Birdsongs weave through the twilight air,
A tranquil symphony, pure and rare.

Ripples shimmer on the serene lake,
Dreams awaken with each breath we take.
The world grows small, just you and I,
In this quiet haven, we learn to fly.

As night unfolds in a velvet cloak,
Stars ignite with a wondrous poke.
Wrapped in comfort, hearts open wide,
In our tranquil escape, we take pride.

The Sound of Solitude

In the silence of night, a gentle hum,
Captured whispers of all that will come.
Moonlight dances, shadows intertwine,
In solitude's embrace, the heart aligns.

Soft footsteps echo on the damp ground,
In the stillness, lost dreams can be found.
A heartbeat lingers, steady and true,
In quiet moments, the world feels new.

Stars sparkle above, secrets untold,
A tapestry woven of dreams so bold.
In the space of calm, our spirits soar,
With each passing breath, we yearn for more.

The sound of solitude, a hymn so sweet,
In the heart's quiet chamber, our worlds meet.
Through silence, we learn, through stillness, we grow,
In the depths of our being, true love we sow.

Soft Revolutions

In the glow of twinkling lights,
We dance beneath the silver moons,
A kaleidoscope of laughing sights,
Joyful hearts to joyous tunes.

Whispers of a newfound cheer,
Lift our spirits, bright and warm,
With every smile, love draws near,
In this moment, we transform.

Colorful banners wave up high,
Cascades of laughter fill the air,
Together, we reach for the sky,
Amongst the dreams that we all share.

With every heartbeat, a soft cheer,
As night unfurls its velvet grace,
In this festive dance, we steer,
Finding joy in every space.

A Silence Within

Amidst the starlit evening's glow,
A quiet hum begins to rise,
In tender moments, joy will flow,
A peaceful hush, a sweet surprise.

Bubbly thoughts and laughter stream,
In every corner, love ignites,
As sparkling dreams begin to beam,
Beneath the shimmering, starry nights.

Close your eyes and feel the breeze,
It carries whispers, soft and light,
The world sways with such sweet ease,
In this festival of delight.

Even in the silence, we sing,
With hearts aglow and spirits free,
For in this quiet, joy will spring,
A gentle pulse of harmony.

The Beauty of Release

As the twilight drapes its shawl,
Radiant colors paint the sky,
We gather round, both great and small,
To celebrate and laugh, oh my!

With every spark, our hopes take flight,
In jubilant swirls of bright confetti,
Each moment glistens, pure delight,
In this dance of time, we're ready.

The sound of music fills the air,
We sway together, side by side,
In shared embraces, we declare,
With love and laughter as our guide.

Let go of worries, feel the bliss,
With open hearts, we claim the night,
The beauty found in every kiss,
As joy envelops, pure and bright.

Gentle Awakening

With dawn's first light, our spirits rise,
A symphony of colors gleam,
In tender rays, the world defies,
The quiet whispers of a dream.

Every flower blooms in grace,
Unfurling petals, bright as suns,
While laughter dances in this place,
Where joy and friendship softly runs.

We celebrate the warmth of day,
With hands held tight, hearts intertwined,
In every moment, bright as play,
The festive spirit we will find.

As nature sings a joyous song,
We gather close, to share and cheer,
In gentle waking, we belong,
Embracing love throughout the year.

Unraveling Chains

Banners flutter in the breeze,
Laughter mingles with the sound,
Joyous hearts break free with ease,
In this festival, dreams abound.

Colors dance, a vivid sight,
Friends unite, a warm embrace,
Underneath the stars so bright,
Every smile a sacred space.

Music swells, the night ignites,
Echoes of a vibrant song,
Life unfolds in pure delights,
Where all souls truly belong.

Time unwinds, and moments blend,
Chains of worry cast aside,
In the magic, hearts shall send,
Wishes high, like stars, our guide.

The Grace of Silence

Amidst the noise, a hush appears,
Holding dreams like whispers slight,
In the stillness, joy adheres,
  Beneath the glow of gentle light.

Candles flicker, shadows play,
Peace enfolds with soft caress,
In this moment, hearts will sway,
  Finding solace, seeking rest.

In the space where silence sings,
Festive souls find their retreat,
Lifted high on whispered wings,
In this grace, the world's complete.

Gathered close, our spirits rise,
In the calm, our wishes bloom,
Underneath vast evening skies,
We celebrate, dispel the gloom.

Inner Landscapes

Painted skies within our souls,
Bursting colors, laughter bright,
Festival of boundless goals,
In our minds, pure delight.

Fields of dreams bloom in our hearts,
Every thought a petal's grace,
Where the music softly starts,
Brings together every face.

Whispers of the past arise,
Flowing gently, sweet and clear,
Every smile a vast surprise,
In this moment, we all cheer.

Mapping journeys yet to come,
Creating worlds with every beat,
In the hum of vibrant drum,
We find joy, our lives complete.

Veils of Tranquility

Softly wrapped in twilight's glow,
Waves of laughter ebb and flow,
Kindred spirits weaving dreams,
In the quiet, joy redeems.

Tapestries of light in air,
Gathered hearts, a bond so rare,
Candles flicker, shadows play,
In this space, we dance and sway.

Veils of calm descend with grace,
Moments cherished, time embraced,
Every whisper, every sound,
Festive notes in peace are found.

Underneath the moon's soft gaze,
Joyful hearts ignite the haze,
Rays of hope through night unfold,
In this stillness, dreams are told.

Freedom's Gentle Breath

Laughter dances in the air,
Bright balloons float everywhere.
Colors burst in joyous gleam,
Life's a vibrant, waking dream.

Music sways, the people cheer,
Echoed joy, the world draws near.
Hearts unite in harmony,
Together, we are wild and free.

Sparkling lights twinkle bright,
Guiding souls through the night.
Every moment's pure delight,
Celebration's shining light.

Whispers soft as morning dew,
In this space, we're born anew.
With each smile, we break the mold,
In this warmth, our dreams unfold.

Subdued Uprising

Underneath the starlit sky,
Gentle laughter floats nearby.
Voices murmur tales of old,
In the night, our dreams unfold.

Candles flicker with sweet grace,
Embers dance in soft embrace.
In the shadows, hearts ignite,
A subdued yet hopeful light.

Colors weave through silent streets,
In our hearts, the rhythm beats.
Every step a quiet claim,
Together, we rise the same.

Under moon's soft, watchful eye,
In our unity, we fly.
With each breath, we find our way,
A quiet night, a festive day.

The Calm Within

In the hush of dawn's first light,
Peaceful whispers take their flight.
Nature sings in softest tones,
In this silence, joy condones.

Every flower blooms with grace,
In their beauty, we find space.
Hope arises with each breeze,
In this calm, our spirits ease.

As the sun begins to rise,
Golden hues paint the skies.
Every heartbeat, a sweet song,
In this moment, we belong.

Beneath the branches, shadows sway,
In this calm, we cherish play.
Harmony within our sight,
Festive souls in pure delight.

Serenity's Breakthrough

Where the river finds its way,
Gentle ripples dance and sway.
In the stillness, colors blend,
Nature's gift, our truest friend.

Sun-kissed faces, laughter plays,
Bringing joy to simple days.
With each heartbeat, life's embrace,
In this moment, find your pace.

Fields of green, their whispers call,
In their reach, we stand so tall.
Freedom's song on every breeze,
In this life, we're meant to seize.

As stars twinkle in the night,
Every soul a twinkling light.
Celebrating all we are,
In this peace, we find our star.

The Art of Letting Go

Balloons float high, they touch the sky,
Laughter spills as moments fly,
We twirl and dance, release our fears,
In this vibrant space, joy draws near.

The music swells, an endless spree,
Friends gather close, a tapestry,
With every laugh, our burdens weigh,
Letting go blooms, it's here to stay.

Cakes and candles, wishes shared,
In this warmth, we've all prepared,
A toast to dreams, new paths we seek,
In letting go, our spirits peak.

As twilight dims, the stars will glow,
In this embrace, we learn to flow,
With every note, our hearts align,
In harmony, we'll always shine.

Echoes in the Void

In the silence, whispers sing,
A festive pulse, a wondrous thing,
Colors dance in shadows laid,
Echoes of joy, never to fade.

Chimes of laughter fill the air,
Moments fleeting, yet we care,
In the void, a spark ignites,
Together, we scale our heights.

Bright lights flicker, sparks arise,
In the wonder, no goodbyes,
Echoes ring of love and cheer,
In this magic, all is clear.

So let the night weave tales anew,
In the void, our hearts break through,
With every echo, a story told,
In festive dreams, we become bold.

Subtle Triumph

A quiet cheer beneath the stars,
Little victories, like fireflies,
In every heart, a whisper glows,
Subtle triumphs, the spirit grows.

Candles lit, a gentle sway,
Each moment cherished, come what may,
In laughter shared, we celebrate,
Life's little wins, we elevate.

With every hug, a bond that's tied,
In the warmth, our dreams abide,
The feast laid out, friendships bloom,
In subtle triumph, we dispel gloom.

So let us raise a glass tonight,
To the joys that feel so right,
In every cheer, a story spun,
Together, we've already won.

Shadows that Speak

Beneath the glow of the harvest moon,
Shadows dance, a festive tune,
They whisper secrets, old and new,
In the night's embrace, we break through.

Stories linger upon the breeze,
With laughter, we find our ease,
Every flicker tells a tale,
In shadows where memories sail.

With lanterns bright, we cast away,
The fleeting worries of the day,
Gathered close, our hearts align,
In shadows that speak, love will shine.

So let the night unfold its grace,
In every smile, we find our place,
Amidst the shadows, we boldly tread,
In this festive glow, all fears shed.

The Liberation of Soft Echoes

Laughter dances in the air,
Bubbles of joy float everywhere.
Colors burst, a vivid sight,
Hearts alight in pure delight.

Voices blend like sweetened song,
Together is where we all belong.
Festive lights twinkle and gleam,
Unity flows like a shared dream.

Friends gather 'round, hand in hand,
Creating magic, a joyful band.
Happiness fills the grandest halls,
In every moment, love enthralls.

Let's embrace this fleeting time,
With every heartbeat, let's chime.
In the echoes, our spirits soar,
Forever free, we want for more.

Whispers of Freedom

In the breeze, whispers take flight,
Stories of hope, pure and bright.
Dancing shadows in twilight glow,
Hints of freedom softly flow.

Banners wave, colors so bold,
Tales of courage wonderfully told.
Hearts unite in rhythmic cheer,
Each laugh a note that we hold dear.

Under the stars, dreams collide,
Awakening joy we cannot hide.
Festivities rise, like a sweet song,
Together we stand, fierce and strong.

Let waves of laughter rise and swell,
In whispered secrets, we can dwell.
For freedom sings, its echoes clear,
Binding us close, year after year.

Silent Revelation

In silence, beauty starts to bloom,
Soft shadows weave, dispelling gloom.
Whispers breathe through the gentle night,
Awakening dreams, casting light.

A spark ignites in every soul,
Hidden wonders that make us whole.
Celebration stirs within the heart,
Unveiling truths that set us apart.

Glances exchanged, a knowing smile,
Time pauses, enriching each mile.
In every corner, magic resides,
Fostering love that forever abides.

Let silence echo with joyful grace,
In this moment, we find our place.
Together we share a radiant glow,
In silent revelation, love will flow.

The Echo of Stillness

Calm descends upon the land,
Nature breathes; it's a soft hand.
In the quiet, joy unfolds,
Catch the warmth, a tale retold.

Stars above begin to twinkle,
Hearts now free, they gently crinkle.
In every pause, new flames ignite,
Illuminating the starry night.

With every echo, spirits rise,
Hidden treasures, a sweet surprise.
Hands interlace, a lovely bond,
A festive night, of which we're fond.

Stillness whispers, songs of cheer,
In our hearts, we hold them near.
With every breath, let laughter sing,
In the echo, joy takes wing.

Freeing the Silent Heart

In twilight's glow, the laughter sings,
Bright colors dance on gentle wings.
Joy fills the air, a sweet embrace,
Together we find our sacred space.

Candles flicker with hope anew,
As dreams awaken, bright and true.
Hearts unspoken beat in time,
To rhythms soft, like subtle chime.

Whispers of love weave through the night,
Stars twinkle with a shining light.
In this festivity, unity gleams,
As we create our sweetest dreams.

With hands entwined, we celebrate,
The joy, the peace, we elevate.
In every smile, a story starts,
Freeing the silent, grateful hearts.

The Unvoiced Journey

Through shimmering paths of gold and green,
The laughter echoes, pure and keen.
Every step a dance, so bright,
In the warmth of this joyous night.

Merry faces, all aglow,
In this fest we let love flow.
Voices join in sweet refrain,
Together we rise, together we gain.

Little moments, big delight,
In the rhythm of pure insight.
Stories shared, a sparkling spree,
Celebrating what we all can be.

With hearts unchained, we wander far,
Guided by our shining star.
The unvoiced journey, a treasure to find,
Together we sail, forever aligned.

Murmurs of the Soul

In the glow of evening's cheer,
Murmurs of the soul draw near.
Threads of warmth in every smile,
Binding us together for a while.

Echoes of laughter fill the air,
Moments cherished, memories rare.
In this fest, our spirits soar,
Finding what we're truly here for.

Every glance, a gentle spark,
Illuminating shadows dark.
With joyous hearts, we intertwine,
In every soul, a love divine.

As music plays, we sway in grace,
Lost in the joy of this sacred space.
Murmurs linger, soft and bright,
A tapestry woven in the night.

Soft Pathways

Beneath the stars, on soft pathways,
We gather close, in bright arrays.
Every moment, a joyous start,
Celebrating life with open heart.

In every hug, in every cheer,
The festive spirit draws us near.
Laughter dances with the breeze,
Carrying hopes that aim to please.

Colors burst like blooms in spring,
Echoes of joy, the songs we sing.
On sparkling trails, we wander bold,
Moments shared are treasures untold.

With spirits high, and hearts so free,
We light the night with harmony.
Soft pathways beckon us to roam,
In this unity, we find our home.

Unnoticed Blossoms

Among the blooms in spring's embrace,
Fragrant whispers find their place.
Colors dance in bright array,
Beneath the sun's warm, golden ray.

In quiet corners, petals spread,
Softly waking, dreams are fed.
A gentle touch, a fleeting glance,
Nature's rhythm, a tender dance.

Joyful laughter fills the air,
Moments cherished, free from care.
Each unnoticed blossom gleams,
In our hearts, they weave their dreams.

Gentle Horizons

Upon the hills where shadows fade,
Golden light begins to wade.
A tapestry of colors bright,
Dancing softly, day and night.

The horizons stretch, alive and wide,
Where hopes and hearts collide in stride.
Joyful echoes fill the sky,
Underneath the clouds that fly.

With every breath, a fresh delight,
Moments linger, pure and light.
In gentle hues, we find our way,
Embraced by warmth of another day.

Hushed Revolutions

In whispered winds of change we find,
A celebration, sweet and kind.
Revolutions bloom in secret places,
With joyful smiles and brightened faces.

The world spins round with hopeful grace,
As hearts unite in this vast space.
Each small step sparks the vast unknown,
Together we rise, no path alone.

In every hush, a promise sings,
Of brighter days and greater things.
Lifted spirits join the song,
In this revolution, we all belong.

Hidden Valleys of Joy

In valleys deep where laughter lies,
Joyful echoes touch the skies.
Hidden paths where dreams abide,
Invite us in, to dance and ride.

Among the trees, a secret glade,
Where memories of joy are made.
The sunbeams kiss the petals low,
In hidden valleys, love will grow.

Come wander through this sacred space,
Find solace in each warm embrace.
In every heartbeat, wonder glows,
In hidden valleys, pure joy flows.

The Freedom of Still Air

In the hush of a twilight glow,
Laughter dances, spirits flow,
Balloons floated, colors bright,
Embracing joy, pure delight.

Whispers of friends, tales unfold,
Under the stars, wonders told,
With each toast, we cheer and sing,
In this moment, hearts take wing.

Candles flicker, shadows play,
A night like this, we wish to stay,
In every smile, a story spun,
Together, we shine, a radiant sun.

As the moon weaves silver thread,
Promises linger, things left unsaid,
The still air breathes a festive sound,
In our laughter, love abounds.

Unspoken Dreams

In the garden where fireflies gleam,
Hope awakens, blooms a dream,
Beneath the arching willow's shade,
A joyous tapestry we've made.

The vibrant hues of laughter rise,
Underneath the painted skies,
In silence shared, connections grow,
A melody of hearts in flow.

With every twirl, and every spin,
A celebration of what's within,
Fulfilled wishes in the night air,
Unity wrapped in a loving care.

In this moment, all feels right,
Stars above, a guiding light,
Together we'll chase unspoken themes,
In the magic of our dreams.

The Liberation of Breath

In the rhythm of the evening breeze,
Every sigh of joy, a sweet release,
Dancing shadows, hearts alight,
Moments shared, pure and bright.

With every laugh, a story spins,
In the air, where freedom begins,
Colors swirl in the twilight's grace,
Finding magic in this space.

Voices blend in the warm embrace,
A symphony of joy, a gentle trace,
As stars wink down with a knowing glance,
In the stillness, we find our dance.

Each heartbeat echoes, loud and free,
A celebration of unity,
The world feels lighter, love's caress,
In the liberation, we find our blessed.

Gentle Murmurs

In the rustling leaves, whispers sigh,
A melody of peace as we lie,
Underneath the starlit dome,
In gentle murmurs, we find home.

The soft embrace of night unfolds,
Stories shared, with laughter bold,
Every moment, cherished dear,
In this haven, we draw near.

With fingers intertwined so tight,
Joy is painted in colors bright,
Every glance a promise made,
In the softness, fears all fade.

As dawn breaks with hues of gold,
Together we greet the tales retold,
With gentle murmurs, hearts align,
In this festive dance, our souls entwine.

www.ingramcontent.com/pod-product-compliance
Ingram Content Group UK Ltd.
Pitfield, Milton Keynes, MK11 3LW, UK
UKHW020104171224
452675UK00013B/1317